25 WAYS TO
STYLE YOUR SCARF

25 WAYS TO
STYLE YOUR SCARF

Lauren Friedman

CHRONICLE BOOKS

SAN FRANCISCO

Published exclusively for Target in 2017 by Chronicle Books LLC.

Manufactured in China

Designed by Allison Weiner
Design assistance by Sarah Higgins

ISBN 978-1-4521-5890-7

10 9 8 7 6 5 4 3 2 1

Library of Congress
Cataloging-in-Publication Data
available under the original title,
50 Ways to Wear a Scarf,
ISBN 978-1-4521-2597-8

Chronicle Books LLC
680 Second Street
San Francisco, California 94107
www.chroniclebooks.com

For my mom and grandma, who made me who I am today.

And to my all-time favorite scarf, pilfered from my mom's closet
and subsequently lost weeks later on New Year's Eve, 2011:
You would have looked great in this book.

CONTENTS

INTRODUCTION

A scarf is more than just an accessory; it has the power to transport your style to another time or place. If you're wearing classic pants with a simple top, pull out a favorite scarf, wrap it into one of the looks found in this book, and suddenly you're a French gamine on the banks of the Seine, a carefree coed skipping class in a convertible, or an anthropologist taking coffee with the local Bedouins. A scarf is the last flourish, the exclamation point to the daily narrative of getting dressed, and it has the ability to truly make an outfit.

My own scarf collection, which I've illustrated throughout this book, is more than just a pile of fabric. My scarves represent a series of stories and memories. The first scarf I ever remember wearing was a purple paisley hand-me-down from my mother's freewheeling single days. When I put it on, I was no longer just a little girl in middle school yearning to grow up. That scarf instantly transformed my daily uniform of a tee shirt and jeans into a look that said, "I'm a young woman with my own style and I march to the beat of my own purple paisley drum!"

I wrote this book to show you the many style possibilities held within a single scarf. If you're tired of doing a simple loop every time you reach for a scarf, fear not—I've illustrated fifty different techniques, and each one says something a little different. Pick and choose depending on your mood, the weather, or the occasion. Try the Audrey (page 86) for a day at the farmers' market, the Hourglass (page 58) for a night painting the town red, or even the Bustier (page 66) for when you're feeling a little naughty. Bring new life to the scarves in the back of your closet, and, above all, don't be afraid to be bold.

–Lauren

THE CLASSIC SCARVES

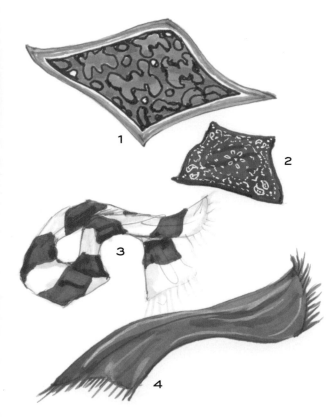

SQUARE SCARVES
1 pashmina or wrap made of cotton, silk, or cashmere
2 bandanna, handkerchief, or small silk square

OBLONG SCARVES
3 heavy knit for winter made of wool or cotton
4 a long swath made of silk, cotton, or cashmere

STORING YOUR SCARVES

Keep your scarves in check! I like to use this type of organizer (available at IKEA) for my collection. Knot each scarf so that the loose ends are hidden and hanging down the back, then organize by type and color. It's a breeze to choose your latest look when all your scarves are visible.

THE LOOKS

★ THE BANDIT ★

For the wily girl on the go, this desperado look
is a runaway success with any old rocker tee.

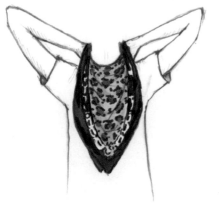

1 With a square scarf folded in half diagonally to form a triangle, gather the two folded corners.

2 Finish by knotting the folded corners together behind your neck.

~ The Rosette ~

A beautiful bloom for any blushing lass, this twist will have everyone stopping to admire the rose at your collar.

1 Drape a long, skinny scarf around the back of your neck so that both ends hang evenly down the front.

2 Starting near your neck, twist the ends together until you are a few inches away from the bottom.

3 Wrap the twist up into a bun on the side of your neck.

4 Tuck the ends underneath, and finish by gently splaying them out like the petals of a flower.

• THE PARIS •

Just how do those Parisian *chéries* achieve that *je ne sais quoi*?
By mastering this elegant style, of course.

1 Fold a square scarf in half diagonally to create a triangle.

2 With the scarf in front of you, wrap the folded corners around your neck, crossing them once in the back.

3 Finish by knotting the folded corners together on top of the scarf in front.

THE MINNIE MOUSE

Our favorite lady mouse proves that there are few things more charming than a big, floppy bow.

Ɛ⟶

1 Place a long scarf at the back of your head at your hairline.

2 Bring the ends forward, tying once above your forehead.

3 Tie the ends into a bow.

4 Finish by adjusting the bow as you see fit.

... The Professor ...

Give this collar-hugging style an A+. Wear it with a crisp button-down shirt, and you'll definitely be on the tenure track.

•••→

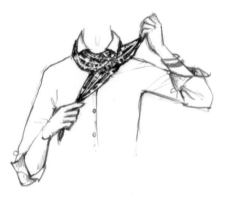

1 Fold a small square scarf in half diagonally to form a triangle. Then, fold over the long edge, in one-inch sections, to form a rectangle. Pop the collar of your button-down and drape the folded scarf around the back of your neck.

2 Wrap the scarf around your neck.

3 Tuck in the ends so the scarf is secure.

4 Fold your collar back down so it rests over the scarf to finish.

< THE PREP >

Any true blue-blood will feel comfortable in this scarf version of the preppy sweater-over-the-shoulder look. Sporting this classic style conjures dreams of summering on Martha's Vineyard and drinking gin and tonics.

1 Fold a large square scarf in half diagonally to form a triangle.

2 Bring the long folded edge of the scarf around the back of your shoulders with the loose corners pointing down your back.

3 Knot the folded corners together at the base of your neck to finish.

~ THE SCULLERY MAID ~

With a jaunty knot on the side of your forehead, this look channels
both hardworking ladies and our favorite late West Coast rapper.
(Tupac, we know you would approve.) No mop or rhyming skills required.

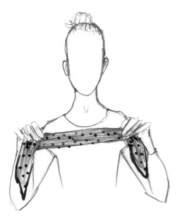

1 Use a small oblong scarf, or fold a small square scarf diagonally into one long length.

2 Place the scarf at the back of your head at your hairline and bring the ends forward.

3 Knot the ends together in the front at a jaunty angle to finish.

The Easy Breezy

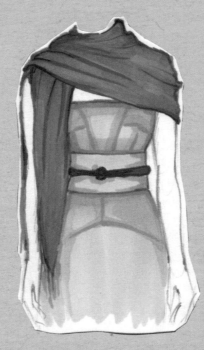

When combined with a strapless cocktail dress,
this effortless look will blow everyone away.

1 Drape a large scarf, wrap, or pashmina around the back of your neck, spreading the scarf over your shoulders.

2 Toss one end over the opposite shoulder to finish.

- THE TOP DOWN -

Reign as queen of the road with this classic head cover.
Cat-eye sunglasses and a convertible are a must.

1 Fold a large square silk scarf in half diagonally to form a triangle.

2 Bring the scarf over your head, with the long folded edge at your forehead and the loose corners pointing down the back of your neck.

3 Cross the folded corners in front beneath your chin.

4 Bring the folded corners back around your neck.

5 Finish by knotting the folded corners together at your neck, tucking the loose corners under the knot.

⚡ THE NEW YORK ⚡

Master winters Big Apple-style with this warm yet trendy look.

�->

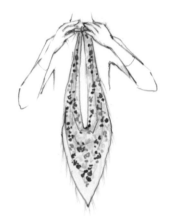  

1 With a large square scarf folded in half diagonally to form a triangle, knot the two folded corners together.

2 Bring the loop over your head, leaving the knotted section slack.

3 Twist the slack to create a second loop.

4 Bring the second loop over your head again.

5 Hiding the knot under the loose corners, finish by fluffing the scarf to create volume and adjust as you like.

Crisscross this uncomplicated tie over your head
and around your neck for a fluttery collar effect.

➤

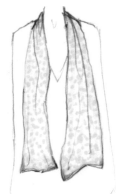

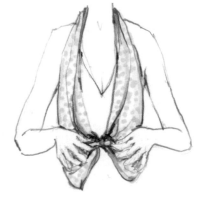

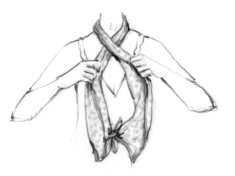

1 Drape an oblong scarf around the back of your neck so the ends hang evenly in front.

2 Knot together the two inside corners.

3 Twist the scarf once to make an X.

4 Flip the scarf over your head, putting your head through the bottom loop created by the X.

5 Finally, adjust as you see fit.

ᴧ THE TIE ᴧ

Once you're practiced in this borrowed-from-the-boys classic, expect the man in your life to come asking for help tying his own. Employ a traditional tie, or go feminine with a long scarf.

1 Drape a long scarf around the back of your neck, letting one end hang longer than the other.

2 Bring the long end over the short end.

3 Wrap the long end under the short end.

4 Bring the long end forward once more, wrapping over the short end.

5 Pull the long end behind the short end and then up through the loop around your neck.

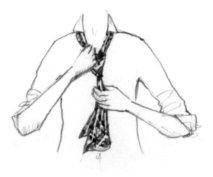

6 Tuck the long end through the front of the knot you created and adjust the length, tightening all the way up to your throat for a more formal look, or leaving it lower for a relaxed vibe.

~ THE KIMONO ~

Pay homage to the elegance of a traditional Japanese kimono with this look. It works well with your best lingerie and kitten heels for an evening in or on top of a formfitting dress for a night out.

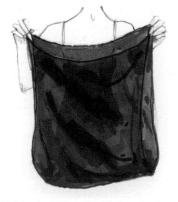

1 Fold a large scarf with lovely drape in half widthwise.

2 On the opposite side of the fold, knot the matching loose corners together, creating two knots.

Pay homage to the elegance of a traditional Japanese kimono with this look. It works well with your best lingerie and kitten heels for an evening in or on top of a formfitting dress for a night out.

1 Fold a large scarf with lovely drape in half widthwise.

2 On the opposite side of the fold, knot the matching loose corners together, creating two knots.

Pay homage to the elegance of a traditional Japanese kimono with this look. It works well with your best lingerie and kitten heels for an evening in or on top of a formfitting dress for a night out.

1 Fold a large scarf with lovely drape in half widthwise.

2 On the opposite side of the fold, knot the matching loose corners together, creating two knots.

3 Insert one arm through the long open end of the scarf and out through one of the short open ends. Bring the scarf behind you and repeat with the other arm, so that one knot comes over your right shoulder and one knot comes over your left.

4 Finally, adjust the scarf so that the knots fall below your arms, allowing the scarf to fall over your shoulders.

The Hourglass

Behold, the fastest way to add definition to your figure.
Choose a belt at least one inch wide for this straightforward style.

 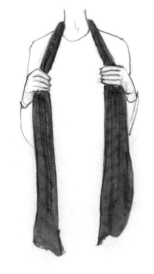 

1 Pick a long rectangular scarf and a belt that go well together.

2 Drape the scarf around the back of your neck so the ends hang evenly in front.

3 With the ends of the scarf lying flat down your front, buckle the belt on top of the scarf. Ensure that you place it at the smallest part of your waist, just below your rib cage.

The Frida

Ms. Kahlo understood the power of a good scarf look. Entwining a scarf with your braided hair simultaneously conveys artistry, strength, and beauty. (Extra points for a strong brow!)

1 Drape a long scarf around the back of your neck underneath hair that has been separated into two sections.

2 Divide each section of hair in three, and incorporate the scarf into one section of hair as you braid to the ends. (If you have "slippery" hair, secure the braid's end with a hair tie.)

3 Repeat on the other side.

4 Bring the braids up around the crown of your head, pinning in place.

5 Finally, tie the ends of the scarf together; fluff the ends to give the impression of a flower. (Or add some flowers of your own!)

17

⇨ THE BUSTIER ⇦

Worn with a high-waisted skirt on a hot day or underneath a jacket for a unique evening look, your favorite large scarf can moonlight as a top in this sexiest of styles. For those girls with gals bigger than an A cup, a strapless bra is recommended.

⊏⟩▷

1 Fold a large scarf lengthwise to your desired width.

2 Place the scarf over your bust and bring the ends around your back.

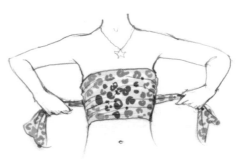

3 Tying once in the back, bring the ends forward.

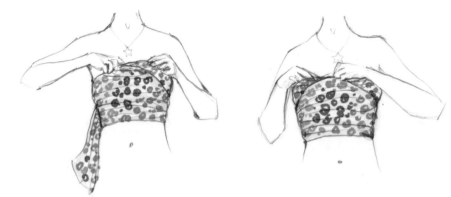

4 Tuck one end into the top of the scarf, ensuring the end is secure.

5 Finish by repeating on the other side. Tucking in in this manner will create a sweetheart neckline effect.

19

THE BOY SCOUT

Earn your merit badge with this wholesome neckerchief.
Worn with crisp neutrals, it pledges adventure—scout's honor!

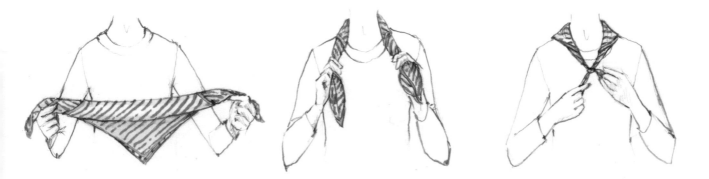

1 Fold a small square cotton bandanna in half diagonally to form a triangle. Then, in one-inch sections, fold over the long edge of the bandanna twice.

2 Drape the bandanna around the back of your neck so that the ends are even in front and the loose corners are hanging down your back.

3 Knot the folded corners together in the front at the base of your throat to finish.

20

The Fan

In old Spain, young ladies looking to be courted used their fans to communicate elaborate secret messages to their suitors. Whatever message you'd like to convey, this ornate look will certainly speak to your style.

1 Drape a large oblong scarf around the back of your neck, letting one end hang much shorter than the other down the front.

2 Form a loose knot on the shorter end.

3 Starting from the bottom, accordion-pleat the longer end until it is even with the knot on the opposite end.

4 On the side closer to the knot, pinch the edge of the pleats with one hand.

5 Pull the pleated end through the knot.

6 Finally, adjust and tighten the knot.

22

❧ THE PEASANT ❧

Add texture, color, and definition with this look.
Over a high-waisted skirt or A-line dress, this method is proof
that style is not synonymous with social class.

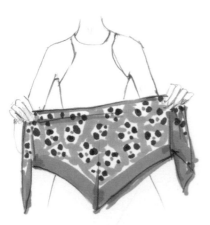 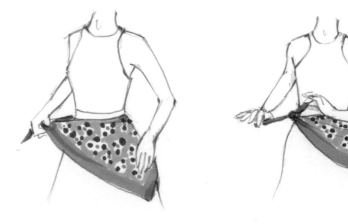

1 Fold a large square scarf in half diagonally to form a triangle.

2 With the loose corners hanging to the side, wrap the scarf around the smallest part of your waist.

3 Finish by knotting the folded corners securely at your side.

{ the bunny ears }

This trendy twist is cute dressed up or dressed down and will have you hopping from one party to the next.

1 Choose a long oblong scarf.

2 Place at the back of your neck, letting one end hang much longer than the other.

3 Wrap the long end twice around your neck.

4 Knot the long end with the short end, hiding the knot beneath the loops when you are finished and letting the "ears" hang down.

24

᮰THE AUDREY᮰

Take inspiration from one of history's most stylish women. When worn with a sweet shirt and flats, this look channels the gamine with confidence and class.

1 Use a small oblong scarf, or fold a square scarf into a long rectangular shape.

2 Place the scarf at the back of your neck, bringing the ends forward.

3 Finish by knotting at the base of your throat.

HISTORY OF THE SCARF

Obviously, scarves were around way before I started dreaming up ways to illustrate them for this book (though at times, that effort did feel quite historical!). There are practically as many ways to tie a scarf as there are manners in which this versatile accessory has gotten tangled up throughout history.

In ancient Egypt, QUEEN NEFERTITI—perhaps the earliest style heroine—sported a scarflike head wrap under her iconic headdress, which was later immortalized in her famous bust.

Meanwhile, in ancient China, military rank was signified by a soldier's hairstyle and dress, including his scarf. Sentry men tied pieces of cloth around their necks in a style similar to the Boy Scout (page 72).

In ancient Rome, men tied linen kerchiefs called *sudariums* (a.k.a. sweat rags) around their necks or belts to wipe away perspiration beneath the hot sun. Apparently Roman women could sweat, too, because they soon adopted the method.

Scarves became articles of chivalry in the Middle Ages of Europe when knights carried the tokens from their ladies into battle. (Can you say romantic?)

QUEEN NEFERTITI

JOSEPHINE

In the seventeenth century, Croatian mercenaries echoed the Chinese tradition of scarves as a marker of rank with soldiers wearing white cotton scarves and officers sporting silk.

Later, during the French Revolution, men and women wore different colored scarves to show their political leanings–*Liberté, Egalié, Fraternité, et Cravates, mais oui!* And while I consider the French to be the epitome of effortless yet elegant scarf style, the French word for scarf, *cravat*, is actually derived from the Croatian word for scarf, *kravata*.

Despite the fact that India had been weaving Kashmir shawls–made of pashmina or cashmere wool, often designed with bright paisley patterns– for centuries, it wasn't until Napoleon brought some

back to his first wife, JOSEPHINE, that the shawl fully implanted itself into fashion history.

The military thread of the scarf's history remained strong entering the twentieth century when, during World War I and World War II, knitting scarves and other necessities for soldiers was deemed patriotic in America. Also during these wars, aviator pilots wore scarves to keep warm in high altitudes and to pad the neck.

However, my award for best-in-flight use of the scarf goes to pioneering pilot AMELIA EARHART, who also had a keen eye for style (she even designed her own clothing line!). Ms. Earhart embodied high-flying panache with her shearling aviator jacket, leather cap, goggles, and flowing silk scarf.

AMELIA EARHART

FLAPPER

Through the twentieth century, the scarf has been tied to fashion and folly alike. Beloved dancer Isadora Duncan was famously killed by her long red scarf when it got caught in the wheel of her convertible. (Keep your Top Down [page 38] tied tight, my dearies!)

The FLAPPERS of the 1920s, known for waistless dresses, cropped hair, and loose morals, tied scarves over their bobs to keep hair polished while dancing the Charleston in the roaring speakeasies of the day.

Toward the end of the decade, in 1928, centuries-old leather goods maker Hermès began to create silk scarves, modeling them after scarves Napoleon's soldiers wore in battle. In countless patterns, designed by innumerable artists and designers, the Hermès scarf has been worn by some of the biggest fashion icons in history, from Audrey Hepburn to Hillary Clinton. My favorite iteration of the Hermès scarf look was when Grace Kelly fashioned one as a sling after she broke her arm in 1956. Trés chic!

Originality is the name of the game when it comes to scarves. Naturally, Jackie O was known for her elegant use of the scarf. But I believe her cousin, Edith Bouvier Beale, better known as Little Edie, was positively smashing with her head scarves. Secured with a brooch and worn with turtlenecks and furs, her scarves are immortalized in the film *Grey Gardens*.

STEVIE NICKS + STEVEN TYLER

MADONNA

Points for originality also go to **STEVIE NICKS** of Fleetwood Mac and **STEVEN TYLER** of Aerosmith, who proved that a rock star is nothing without a scarf—or twelve—swaying under the mic.

On the silver screen, notable scarf mentions go to Faye Dunaway in the 1967 film *Bonnie and Clyde* (the *ultimate* Bandit [page 16] inspiration) and Diane Keaton in 1977's *Annie Hall*, who made Woody Allen fall in love with her borrowed-from-the-boys suits, hats, and drape-y scarves.

In the '80s, pop princess **MADONNA** corralled her epic perm with a subversive version of the Scullery Maid (page 34) during her infamous "Like a Virgin" days.

Harkening back to an earlier time, the cashmere pashmina, as prevalent in the 1990s as the nylon Prada backpack, was dubbed a "cashmiracle" by Carrie Bradshaw, played by Sarah Jessica Parker, in a 1999 episode of *Sex and the City*.

Even now as we enter the second decade of the twenty-first century, the scarf shows no evidence of fading away. The late, great author and screenwriter Nora Ephron extolled their concealing virtues in her 2006 book *I Feel Bad About My Neck*, while Alexander McQueen's much-copied silk skull scarves whipped up a frenzy of a trend, still appearing on celebrities and fans alike.

CROSS-REFERENCE INDEX

ACKNOWLEDGMENTS

THANK YOU to Laura Lee and Allison at Chronicle Books—their patience and encouragement brought this book to life in ways I couldn't have imagined. To Greer, for her incredible modeling skills (and her constant supply of cookie dough). To Jonas and Cullen, for giving me the means to turn my ideas into reality. To Torie, for being an eye or ear to rely on and a studio-mate to look up to. To Laura, Ashlea, Jana, Jordan, Safia, and Katie, because our friendships are the spark I couldn't live without. To my brother, Alex, who had to live with me while I made this book, and whose coaching and tough love kept my gas tank full the whole way through. To my parents, Larry and Mary, for their unending support and utter lack of pretentiousness when it comes to "things that are a big deal"—you keep my feet on the ground where they belong. To Zoe, the best damn dog to ever sport a scarf. Last but not least, to my grandmother Enid, who always seems to cosmically come through. While visiting her just days before finishing the final outline of this book, I unearthed a treasure trove of old scarves and vintage "How to Tie a Scarf" pamphlets full of styles I had never seen before. These last-minute finds inspired some of my favorite looks in this book: the Fan and the XX. In the same way a scarf adds that final flourish, I credit my grandmother's creative spirit for the finishing touches on this book.